AMERICA
COOKING

Copyright © 1997 Tripart, Ltd.

MODERN PUBLISHING

A Division of Unisystems, Inc. / New York, New York 10022

Printed in the U.S.A.

BUTTERNUT SQUASH SOUP

1 medium yellow onion, peeled
    and chopped
1 medium leek (white end),
    washed and sliced
1 large carrot, peeled and
    sliced thin
4 tbs (60 ml) butter, margarine,
    or oil
1 tsp (5 ml) coriander
1 tsp (5 ml) ground cumin
pinch IMPERIAL Granulated
    Sugar
1 medium-large butternut
    squash, peeled, seeded, and
    cut into 1–2-inch chunks
4 cups (960 ml) chicken broth,
    regular or low-sodium
½ cup (120 ml) Fumé Blanc wine,
    optional
salt and white pepper to taste
sour cream and minced fresh
    parsley for garnish,
    optional

In soup kettle, sauté onion, leek, carrot in butter, margarine, or oil over medium heat until limp. Stir in coriander, cumin, Imperial Granulated Sugar and continue to sauté, stirring occasionally, about 5 minutes. Add chopped squash and chicken stock. Cook until squash is tender, about 20 minutes. In food processor or blender, purée mixture until smooth. Add more chicken broth and wine (optional) for desired consistency. Return puréed mixture to pot, taste for seasonings, and add more coriander and cumin, if desired. Stir well and simmer 10 minutes. Add salt and white pepper to taste. Garnish with spoonful of sour cream sprinkled with parsley. Serves 4.

Note: Squash will be easier to peel, if, after seeding and cutting into large pieces, it is processed on HIGH in microwave with 2 tbs water, covered. If necessary, cool heated squash in cold water and proceed to peel.

Approximate nutritional analysis per serving:
Calories 212, Protein 7 g,
Carbohydrates 19 g, Fat 13 g,
Cholesterol 0 mg, Sodium 941 mg

Opposite:
Old-Fashioned Split Pea Soup

OLD-FASHIONED SPLIT PEA SOUP

1 cup (240 ml) split peas
1 ham bone *or* ½ cup ham,
    cubed, with excess fat
    removed
1 carrot, grated
2 medium onions, minced
1 potato, grated
¼ cup (60 ml) celery, diced
¼ cup (60 ml) green pepper,
    finely chopped
1 tsp (5 ml) IMPERIAL
    Granulated Sugar
salt and pepper to taste
additional pieces of ham, diced

Cover split peas with 6 cups boiling water; let soak for 1 hour. Add ham bone, carrot, onion, potato, celery, green pepper, and Imperial Granulated Sugar. Simmer 30–40 minutes or until peas are tender. Season with salt and pepper. Add water if needed; simmer 5–10 minutes longer. Pour into soup bowls; garnish with diced ham. Serves 4.

Approximate nutritional analysis per serving:
Calories 260, Protein 17 g,
Carbohydrates 41 g, Fat 4 g,
Cholesterol 11 mg, Sodium 230 mg

CHICKEN VEGETABLE DUMPLING SOUP

1 cup (240 ml) onion, chopped,
½ cup (120 ml) celery, chopped
½ cup (120 ml) red pepper,
    chopped
2 cloves garlic, minced, divided
1 tbs (15 ml) FLEISCHMANN'S
    Margarine
2 - 13¾ oz cans (825 ml)
    COLLEGE INN Lower Salt
    Chicken Broth
½ lb (230 g) cooked chicken,
    shredded
1 cup (240 ml) fresh green beans,
    cut
1 cup (240 ml) carrots, sliced
1 - 14½ oz can (435 g) low-salt
    stewed tomatoes
1¼ cups (295 ml) water
½ cup (120 ml) Regular, Quick,
    or Instant CREAM OF
    WHEAT Cereal
¼ cup (60 ml) parsley, chopped
2 eggs, slightly beaten

In 4-qt saucepan, over medium heat, cook ¾ cup onion, celery, pepper, and half the garlic in margarine until tender. Stir in chicken broth, chicken, beans, carrots, and stewed tomatoes; cover and simmer for 20 minutes.

In medium saucepan, over high heat, heat water, ¼ cup onion, and remaining garlic to a boil; slowly stir in cereal. Cook and stir in parsley and eggs. Drop mixture by tablespoonfuls into simmering soup; cover. Cook over low heat for 10 minutes or until dumplings are cooked. Serves 8.

Approximate nutritional analysis per serving:
Calories 176, Protein 12 g,
Carbohydrates 12 g, Fat 6 g,
Cholesterol 81 mg, Sodium 382 mg

PEAR WALDORF SALAD MOLD

PEAR MOLD:
2 fresh USA Pears
1 - 3 oz pkg. (90 g) lemon flavor
    gelatin
½ tsp (3 ml) salt
1 cup (240 ml) boiling water
¾ cup (180 ml) cold water
½ cup (120 ml) red grapes,
    halved and seeded
¼ cup (60 ml) celery, chopped
¼ cup (60 ml) walnuts, chopped
Creamy Waldorf Dressing
    (below)
pear slices and grapes
    for garnish

CREAMY WALDORF DRESSING:
¾ cup (180 ml) mayonnaise
½ tsp (3 ml) lemon peel, grated
1 tbs (15 ml) sugar
¼ cup (60 ml) heavy cream,
    whipped
chopped walnuts for garnish

Core and dice pears, but do not peel. Dissolve lemon gelatin and salt in boiling water. Add cold water. Chill until partially set. Add pears, grapes, celery, and walnuts. Pour into 4-cup mold and chill until firm. Unmold and serve with Creamy Waldorf Dressing. Garnish with pear slices and grapes. Serves 6.

Creamy Waldorf Dressing: Combine mayonnaise, lemon peel, and sugar. Fold in whipped cream. Serve, garnished with chopped nuts. Yields 1¼ cups.

Approximate nutritional analysis per serving of pear mold:
Calories 83, Protein 1 g,
Carbohydrates 14 g, Fat 3 g,
Cholesterol 0 mg, Sodium 190 mg

Approximate nutritional analysis per 2 tbs serving of dressing:
Calories 121, Protein 1 g,
Carbohydrates 18 g, Fat 7 g,
Cholesterol 4 mg, Sodium 244 mg

OVEN-FRIED CHICKEN

2½–3½ lb (1.1–1.6 kg) cut-up
   broiler-fryer chicken
1 tbs (15 ml) margarine
⅔ cup (160 ml) BISQUICK
   Reduced Fat Baking Mix
1½ tsp (8 ml) paprika
1¼ tsp (6 ml) salt
¼ tsp (1 ml) pepper

Heat oven to 425°F (220°C). Remove
skin from chicken. Heat margarine in
rectangular pan, 13x9x2 inches, in oven
until melted. Mix baking mix, paprika,
salt, and pepper; coat chicken. Place
pieces, meaty sides down, in pan (pan
and margarine should be hot). Bake 35
minutes. Turn; bake about 15 minutes
longer or until done. Serves 6.

   Mexican Oven-Fried Chicken:
Decrease baking mix to ½ cup. Add 2
tbs yellow cornmeal and 1–2 tbs chili
powder.

Approximate nutritional analysis per serving
Oven-Fried Chicken: Calories 230,
Protein 27 g, Carbohydrates 9 g, Fat 10 g,
Cholesterol 80 mg, Sodium 700 mg

Approximate nutritional analysis per serving
Mexican Oven-Fried Chicken: Calories 220,
Protein 27 g, Carbohydrates 8 g, Fat 9 g,
Cholesterol 80 mg, Sodium 670 mg

Oven-Fried Chicken

ROAST TURKEY WITH FENNEL-CORNBREAD STUFFING

(Closed Foil Method)

STUFFING:

2 tbs (30 ml) olive oil
4 onions, sliced very thin
6 cloves garlic, minced
2 fennel bulbs, chopped,
    reserve fronds
2 lbs (910 g) fresh mushrooms,
    1 lb sliced, 1 lb chopped
4 cups (960 ml) dry French bread
    cubes
5 cups (1.2 l) cornbread cubes,
    dry
2–3 tsp (10–15 ml) thyme leaves
1 tsp (5 ml) sage
1 cup (240 ml) chopped Italian
    parsley
½ cup (120 ml) sun-dried
    tomatoes, chopped and
    soaked in:
    ½ cup (120 ml) kosher sherry
1 tsp (5 ml) crushed fennel seeds
freshly ground pepper, to taste
2 cups (480 ml) kosher chicken
    broth

TURKEY:

1 - 18–20 lb (8–9 kg) turkey, fresh
    or completely defrosted, neck
    and giblet reserved
1 fennel bulb, sliced into 6 pieces,
    reserve fronds
2 carrots, peeled and quartered
1 onion, quartered
1 tbs (15 ml) vegetable oil
2 cups (480 ml) kosher chicken
    broth (additional broth may
    be needed for gravy)

8 cloves garlic, crushed
1 cup (240 ml) apricot preserves
1–2 tbs (15–30 ml) soy sauce
1 tsp (5 ml) thyme leaves, dried
freshly ground pepper
½ cup (120 ml) orange juice
½ cup (120 ml) kosher sherry
½ tsp (3 ml) cornstarch

Stuffing: Heat oil in a large skillet. Sauté onions, garlic, and fennel over low heat until soft, about 10 minutes. Add chopped and sliced mushrooms. Sauté 2 minutes more. Transfer vegetables to a large bowl and set aside. Add dry cubes of bread, herbs, chopped sun-dried tomatoes with their soaking liquid, fennel seeds, and freshly ground pepper. Lightly toss ingredients together. Add chicken broth and toss again, lightly. Set stuffing aside while preparing turkey.

Turkey: Preheat oven to 400°F (205°C). Rinse the turkey well, trim all visible fat, pat dry, and stuff the cavity loosely with stuffing, allowing for expansion. Stuff the neck area and secure with neck skin. Put any remaining stuffing in oven proof baking dish and set aside.

In the bottom of a large roasting pan, arrange a bed of the fennel slices, reserved fronds, and carrot and onion pieces. Gently place the turkey on top, breast side up. Rub oil all over the bird. Pour 1 cup of the broth in the pan, place pan in hot oven, and roast turkey for 30 minutes to seal in the juices.

Meanwhile, prepare the basting glaze; combine the garlic, preserves, soy sauce, thyme, pepper, 1 cup broth, and

orange juice in a bowl and set aside.

After 30 minutes, remove or pull turkey out on rack, brush on glaze, covering entire surface. Create a tent with 2 large pieces of foil that allow 3–4 inches of air space so that you can open to baste and then reclose. Return covered turkey to oven and reduce to 350°F (180°C). Roast the turkey for 4 hours, basting every hour with basting mixture and pan juices. After 4 hours, uncover the turkey to allow it to brown further. Bake 1 more hour, basting 2–3 times (approximately 5 hours total cooking time). If you have extra stuffing to bake, stir in a bit of broth or pan juices, loosely cover, and bake for the last 40–50 minutes.

Transfer the turkey to a heated platter, cover loosely, and allow it to rest 15–20 minutes before carving. While the turkey rests, strain and de-fat the pan juices—you should have 4 cups (add broth if necessary). Place in a saucepan. Heat to simmer.

In a small bowl, combine sherry and cornstarch. Then whisk into saucepan, simmer 5–7 minutes, add salt and pepper to taste, and serve with turkey. Serves 18.

Approximate nutritional analysis per serving:
Calories 998, Protein 131 g,
Carbohydrates 46 g, Fat 28 g,
Cholesterol 343 mg, Sodium 604 mg

Courtesy of the Empire Kosher Poultry Test Kitchens.

CHICKEN BREASTS WITH ORANGE-LIME SAUCE

2 whole chicken breasts, skinned, boned, and cut in half
salt and white pepper
7 tbs (105 ml) butter, divided
1 cup (240 ml) orange juice
1 tbs (15 ml) lime juice
¼ tsp (1 ml) grated orange peel
⅔ cup (160 ml) BLUE DIAMOND Sliced Natural Almonds, toasted

Lightly flatten chicken breasts. Season with salt and pepper. Sauté breasts in 1 tbs butter, 2–3 minutes on each side or until cooked through. Remove and keep warm. Add orange juice, lime juice, and orange peel to pan. Simmer over high heat until mixture thickens to a syrupy consistency. Add ½ tsp salt and ⅛ tsp pepper. Over low heat, whisk in remaining 6 tbs butter until sauce is thick and glossy. Add almonds and pour over chicken. Serves 4.

Approximate nutritional analysis per serving:
Calories 474, Protein 32 g,
Carbohydrates 11 g, Fat 35 g,
Cholesterol 127 mg, Sodium 69 mg

Chicken Breasts with
Orange-Lime Sauce

FRIED CHICKEN OLD BAY STYLE

1 - 2½–3 lb (1.1–1.4 kg) chicken, cut up
1 cup (240 ml) flour
¼ cup (60 ml) OLD BAY Seasoning
2 cups (480 ml) cooking oil
2 tbs (30 ml) water
1 egg, beaten

Wash chicken and pat dry. Mix flour and Old Bay Seasoning. Heat cooking oil in a large skillet. In mixing bowl, combine water and egg. Dip chicken in egg mixture, then in flour (a few pieces at a time). Fry over medium heat until golden brown, about 20 minutes on each side. Serves 4.

Approximate nutritional analysis per serving:
Calories 413, Protein 58 g,
Carbohydrates 3 g, Fat 17 g,
Cholesterol 177 mg, Sodium 171 mg

SAVORY MUSHROOM-STUFFED STEAK

1 tbs (15 ml) olive oil
1 cup (240 ml) finely chopped fresh mushrooms
¼ cup (60 ml) minced shallots or green onions
1 tbs (15 ml) dry red wine
¼ tsp (1 ml) salt
¼ tsp (1 ml) dried thyme leaves
¼ tsp (1 ml) pepper
3 lbs (1.4 g) boneless beef tip sirloin steak, cut 2 inches thick

Heat oil in heavy nonstick skillet over medium-high heat. Add mushrooms and shallots; cook 4–5 minutes or until vegetables are tender, stirring occasionally. Add wine and cook until evaporated. Stir in salt, thyme, and pepper. Remove from heat; cool thoroughly. Meanwhile trim excess fat from beef top sirloin steak. To cut pocket in steak, make horizontal cut through center of steak, parallel to surface of meat, approximately 1 inch from each side. Cut to, but not through, opposite side. Spoon cooled stuffing into pocket, spreading evenly. Secure opening with wooden picks. Place steak on rack in broiler pan so surface of meat is 4–5 inches from heat. Broil 26–32 minutes for rare to medium, turning once. Place on warm serving platter. Cover with aluminum foil tent and allow to stand 10–15 minutes. Remove wooden picks. Trim excess fat from steak; carve steak into ½-inch thick slices. Serves 12.

Note: A boneless beef top sirloin steak will yield 4 - 3 oz (90 g each) cooked, trimmed servings per lb (455 g).

Approximate nutritional analysis per serving:
Calories 180, Protein 26 g,
Carbohydrates 1 g, Fat 7 g,
Cholesterol 76 mg, Sodium 102 mg

Courtesy of the National Livestock and Meat Board.

Opposite: Spicy Pepper Steak

SPICY PEPPER STEAK

1 lb (455 g) sirloin tip beef steak, cut ½ inch thick
2 tbs (30 ml) soy sauce
1 tbs (15 ml) cornstarch
¼ cup (60 ml) water
½ cup (120 ml) HEINZ Chili Sauce
¼ tsp (1 ml) salt
⅛ tsp (.5 ml) red pepper
⅛ tsp (.5 ml) black pepper
1 medium onion, halved, sliced
2 tbs (30 ml) vegetable oil, divided
3 large bell peppers (green, red, yellow, or combination), cut into ¼-inch strips

Slice steak diagonally across the grain into ¼x2-inch pieces. Sprinkle soy sauce over steak and toss to coat; set aside. In small bowl, combine cornstarch and water; stir in chili sauce, salt, red pepper, and black pepper and set aside.

In large skillet or wok, stir-fry onion in 1 tbs oil 1 minute. Add bell peppers and stir-fry until peppers are crisp-tender, about 3 minutes; remove. Stir-fry steak in remaining 1 tbs oil 2 minutes; stir in chili sauce mixture. Simmer 1 minute until thickened, stirring constantly. Stir in pepper mixture; heat. Serve with rice, if desired. Serves 4.

Approximate nutritional analysis per serving:
Calories 379, Protein 37 g,
Carbohydrates 21 g, Fat 3 g,
Cholesterol 101 mg, Sodium 1182 mg

PARTY BARBECUE

3–3½ lb (1.4–1.6 kg) beef brisket
¼ cup (60 ml) water
2 tbs (30 ml) liquid smoke
½ tsp (3 ml) garlic salt
¼ tsp (1 ml) pepper
2½ cups (590 ml) HEINZ Tomato Ketchup
⅓ cup (80 ml) firmly packed brown sugar
2 tbs (30 ml) Worcestershire sauce
1 tbs (15 ml) HEINZ Apple Cider Vinegar
1 tsp (5 ml) prepared mustard
½ tsp (3 ml) garlic salt
½ tsp (3 ml) onion salt
¼ tsp (1 ml) black pepper
¼ tsp (1 ml) red pepper
semi-hard rolls or sandwich buns

Place beef and next 4 ingredients in Dutch oven. Cover tightly; cook over low heat 2 hours. Remove beef; reserve ½ cup meat juices. Allow beef to cool slightly for easier slicing. Thinly slice beef diagonally across the grain. In same Dutch oven, combine reserved meat juices, ketchup, and remaining ingredients except rolls; simmer covered, 5 minutes. Add sliced beef; heat. Serve in rolls. Serves 12.

Approximate nutritional analysis per serving w/o bread: Calories 286, Protein 33 g, Carbohydrates 19 g, Fat 8 g, Cholesterol 92 mg, Sodium 819 mg

CHILI-ROASTED SIRLOIN WITH CORN PUDDING

CORN PUDDING:

1 - 20 oz bag (600 g) frozen whole kernel corn, defrosted
1 small onion, quartered
2 cups (480 ml) 2% milk
2 eggs, beaten
1 - 8½ oz box (255 g) corn muffin mix
½ tsp (3 ml) salt
4 oz (120 g) shredded cheddar cheese
1 cup (240 ml) thinly sliced Romaine lettuce
½ cup (120 ml) julienned radishes

SIRLOIN:

2 large garlic cloves, crushed
2 tsp (10 ml) chili powder
¾ tsp (4 ml) dried oregano leaves, crushed
½ tsp (3 ml) ground cumin
3 lb (1.4 kg) boneless beef top sirloin steak, cut 2 inches thick
salt and pepper to taste

Corn Pudding: Combine corn and onion in food processor bowl fitted with steel blade; cover and process until corn is broken but not puréed, scraping side of bowl as necessary. Add milk and eggs; process until just blended. Add muffin mix and salt; process only until mixed. Pour mixture into greased 11¾x7½-inch baking dish. Bake 45–50 minutes or until outside crust is golden brown. Sprinkle cheese on top and broil until cheese is melted and top is crusty. Top with Romaine lettuce and radishes before serving. Serves 8.

Combine garlic, chili powder, oregano, and cumin; press into both sides of beef top sirloin steak. Place steak on rack in shallow roasting pan. Do not add water. Do not cover. Roast in moderate, 350°F (180°C), oven to desired doneness. Allow 16–20 minutes per lb (455 g) for rare. Remove steak when meat thermometer registers 135°F (57°C) for rare. Season with salt and pepper to taste. Cover steak with aluminum foil tent and allow to stand 10 minutes. Thick-cut steaks will continue to rise approximately 5°F (3°C) in temperature to 140°F (60°C) for rare. Trim excess fat from steak; carve into thin slices. Serve with Corn Pudding. Serves 8.

Note: A boneless beef top sirloin steak will yield 4 - 3 oz (90 g each) cooked, trimmed servings per lb (455 g).

Approximate nutritional analysis per serving Corn Pudding: Calories 270, Protein 10 g, Carbohydrates 39 g, Fat 9 g, Cholesterol 81 mg, Sodium 545 mg

Approximate nutritional analysis per 3 oz cooked, trimmed serving meat: Calories 180, Protein 26 g, Carbohydrates 1 g, Fat 7 g, Cholesterol 76 mg, Sodium 61 mg

Courtesy of the National Livestock and Meat Board.

COWBOY BARBECUED RIBS

5 lbs (2.3 kg) pork spareribs
1 cup (240 ml) water
⅓ cup (80 ml) butter or
  margarine
2 tbs (30 ml) fresh lemon juice
¼ cup (60 ml) dry mustard
¼ cup (60 ml) chili powder
1 tbs (15 ml) sugar
1 tbs (15 ml) paprika
2 tsp (10 ml) salt
1 tsp (5 ml) onion powder
1 tsp (5 ml) garlic powder
¼ tsp (1 ml) cayenne pepper

Place spareribs on broiler pan. Cover with foil. Roast at 400°F (205°C) for 1½ hours. Meanwhile, combine remaining ingredients in medium saucepan; mix well. Bring to boil. Reduce heat; simmer for 30 minutes. Brush sauce on ribs. Broil 5 inches from heat for 7–10 minutes on each side. Serve ribs with additional sauce. Serves 6.

Approximate nutritional analysis per serving:
Calories 706, Protein 45 g,
Carbohydrates < 1 g, Fat 55 g,
Cholesterol 204 mg, Sodium 1126 mg

Courtesy of the National Pork Producers Council.

Cowboy Barbecued Ribs

CRANBERRY GLAZED TURKEY BREAST

1 - 6 lb (2.7 kg) NORBEST Turkey Breast, bone in
1 cup (240 ml) jellied cranberry sauce
1 cup (240 ml) orange marmalade
2 tsp (10 ml) dry mustard
2 tsp (10 ml) lemon juice
½ tsp (3 ml) ground cloves

In small roasting pan, fitted with meat rack, place turkey breast on rack. Bake at 325°F (165°C) 1¾–2 hours or until meat thermometer inserted in thickest part of breast reaches 170–175°F (78–79°C).

In small saucepan, over medium heat, combine cranberry sauce, marmalade, mustard, lemon juice, and cloves. Cook 4–5 minutes or until sauce is smooth. Brush 2–3 tbs sauce over turkey breast during last 20 minutes of baking. Serve remaining sauce over turkey slices. Serves 10.

Approximate nutritional analysis per serving: Calories 476, Protein 54 g, Carbohydrates 32 g, Fat 14 g, Cholesterol 138 mg, Sodium 144 mg

SPRINGTIME HAM WITH RHUBARB SAUCE

3–4 lb (1.4–1.8 kg) boneless fully-cooked smoked ham half
½ cup (120 ml) water
1 - 16 oz pkg. (480 g) frozen cut rhubarb, defrosted
***or* 3 cups (720 ml) sliced fresh rhubarb**
1¼ cups (295 ml) sugar
⅓ cup (80 ml) orange juice
2 tsp (10 ml) grated orange peel
¾ tsp (4 ml) dry mustard
1 cinnamon stick

Do not preheat oven. Place smoked ham half, straight from the refrigerator, on rack in shallow roasting pan. Add water. Insert meat thermometer into thickest part of ham, not touching fat. Cover pan tightly with aluminum foil, leaving thermometer dial exposed. Roast in slow, 325°F (165°C), oven until meat thermometer registers 135°F (57°C), approximately 19–23 minutes per lb (455 g).

Meanwhile, combine rhubarb, sugar, orange juice, orange peel, mustard, and cinnamon stick in large saucepan. Bring to a boil; reduce heat to medium. Cook, uncovered, 15 minutes, stirring occasionally. Remove and discard cinnamon stick. Remove aluminum foil and spoon small amount of sauce over ham 15 minutes before end of cooking time. Remove ham when meat thermometer registers 135°F (57°C). Cover ham with aluminum foil tent and allow to stand approximately 10 minutes or until meat thermometer registers 140°F (60°C). Serve ham with remaining sauce. Serves 12–20.

Note: A boneless fully-cooked smoked ham half will yield 4–5 - 3 oz (90 g each) cooked, trimmed servings per lb (455 g).

Approximate nutritional analysis per serving: Calories 193, Protein 18 g, Carbohydrates 19 g, Fat 5 g, Cholesterol 45 mg, Sodium 1025 mg

Courtesy of the National Livestock and Meat Board.

Opposite:
Springtime Ham
with Rhubarb Suace

PORK AND TOMATO SAUERKRAUT

2 tbs (30 ml) oil
2 cloves garlic, minced
4 center cut pork chops
1 - 6 oz can (180 ml) LIBBY'S
    Tomato Paste
1 cup (240 ml) sour cream
¼ cup (60 ml) brown sugar
1 - 29 oz can (870 g) sauerkraut

Heat oil in skillet, sauté garlic; add pork chops and brown well. In 2-qt casserole blend tomato paste, sour cream, and brown sugar. Stir in sauerkraut. Arrange pork chops on top of sauerkraut. Bake uncovered for 20 minutes at 350°F (180°C) or until meat is done. Serves 4.

Approximate nutritional analysis per serving:
Calories 475, Protein 28 g,
Carbohydrates 33 g, Fat 26 g,
Cholesterol 96 mg, Sodium 1742 mg

Pork and Tomato Sauerkraut

PORK TENDERLOIN WITH APPLE WINE SAUCE

1 ¼ lbs (570 g) pork tenderloin
2 ½ tbs (38 ml) vegetable oil
1 small onion, chopped
2 tbs (30 ml) butter
¾ cup (180 ml) white or blush
wine
10 ½ oz (315 g) COMSTOCK
Apple Filling or Topping
salt and pepper to taste

Preheat oven to 375°F (190°C). Place pork on rack in roasting pan. Brush with oil and cook 45–55 minutes or until internal temperature reaches 155–160°F (68–71°C).

Sauté onion in butter over medium-low heat until soft and transparent. Stir in wine. Bring to gentle boil and boil 3–5 minutes until reduced to ½ cup. Stir in Apple Filling. Transfer to a food processor or blender and process until smooth. Add salt and pepper to taste. Stir in remaining oil. Use as a basting sauce for tenderloin, basting every 10 minutes.

When roast reaches 155–160°F (68–71°C), remove from oven and tent with foil. Return apple mixture to saucepan and bring to a boil for 2 minutes. Slice pork and serve with apple mixture. Serves 4.

Approximate nutritional analysis per serving:
Calories 380, Protein 29 g,
Carbohydrates 14 g, Fat 20 g,
Cholesterol 99 mg, Sodium 138 mg

OLD BAY CATFISH

2 lbs (910 g) catfish
½–1 cup (120–240 ml) yellow
cornmeal
3 tbs (45 ml) butter or margarine
1 ½ tbs (25 ml) OLD BAY
Seasoning
1 tsp (5 ml) paprika
1 tsp (5 ml) parsley flakes
½ tsp (3 ml) garlic salt

Old Bay Catfish

Roll catfish in cornmeal. In large frying pan, melt butter. Add catfish to pan. Shake Old Bay Seasoning over catfish until covered. Sprinkle paprika, parsley flakes, and garlic salt over catfish. Fry until golden brown, about 10–15 minutes each side. Serves 6.

Approximate nutritional analysis per serving:
Calories 279, Protein 29 g,
Carbohydrates 13 g, Fat 11 g,
Cholesterol 88 mg, Sodium 273 mg

NORTHWEST SALMON WITH HAZELNUT AND JUNIPER BERRY SAUCE

**4 - ½ lb (230 g each) salmon
    steaks**
¼ cup (60 ml) hazelnuts, broken
3 juniper berries, crushed
½ cup (120 ml) brandy
½ cup (120 ml) cream
salt

Sauté salmon steak in nonstick pan.
Remove from pan. Add hazelnuts and
juniper berries, then deglaze with
brandy. When mixture is reduced and
alcohol is gone, add cream. Cook until
thickened. Salt to taste. Pour over warm
salmon steak and enjoy! Serves 4.

Approximate nutritional analysis per serving:
Calories 538, Protein 47 g,
Carbohydrates 12 g, Fat 30 g,
Cholesterol 165 mg, Sodium 112 mg

Courtesy of the American Hazelnut
Board

**Northwest Salmon with
Hazelnut and Juniper Berry Sauce**

SHRIMPOREE CREOLE

1 lb (455 g) shrimp, uncooked
½ cup (120 ml) chopped onion
½ cup (120 ml) chopped green
pepper
2 cloves garlic, minced
¼ cup (60 ml) minced celery
3 tbs (45 ml) butter, margarine,
or oil
1 tbs (15 ml) all-purpose flour
1 - 1 lb can (455 g) sliced stewed
tomatoes
⅛ tsp (.5 ml) dried thyme
1 bay leaf
½ tsp (3 ml) IMPERIAL
Granulated Sugar
1 tsp (5 ml) Worcestershire sauce
several whole allspice berries
salt and pepper
minced parsley
hot, freshly cooked rice

Cook shrimp. Remove shells and devein. To make Creole sauce, sauté onion, green pepper, garlic, celery in butter until limp; add flour, cook, and stir until flour is light tan. Add all other ingredients except parsley and rice. Cook until sauce is thickened. Taste for salt and pepper and add more if needed. Stir in parsley. Serve over hot, freshly cooked rice. Serves 4.

Approximate nutritional analysis per serving:
Calories 361, Protein 28 g,
Carbohydrates 39 g, Fat 10 g,
Cholesterol 221 mg, Sodium 1192 mg

Shrimporee Creole

SEAFOOD SUPREME

½ cup (120 ml) **margarine**
1 cup (240 ml) **chopped green**
    pepper
1 cup (240 ml) **chopped celery**
1 medium **onion, chopped**
1½ lbs (685 g) **fresh shrimp,**
    shelled
3 tbs (45 ml) **flour**
3 cups (720 ml) **milk**
1 cup (240 ml) **mayonnaise**
2 tbs (30 ml) **mustard**
3 tbs (45 ml) **Worcestershire**
    sauce
2–3 tbs (30–45 ml) **OLD BAY**
    Seasoning to taste
1½ lbs (685 g) **sea legs (imitation**
    crab meat)
½ cup (120 ml) **cracker crumbs**
OLD BAY Seasoning for topping

In a large skillet, melt margarine; add green pepper, celery, onion, and shrimp; sauté over medium heat until vegetables are tender and shrimp is done. Add flour to skillet and stir until flour is absorbed. Add milk, stirring until mixture thickens. Take skillet off heat and cool.

    Preheat oven to 350°F (180°C). In a large 6-qt casserole dish, add mayonnaise, mustard, Worcestershire sauce, Old Bay Seasoning, and sea legs. Mix well. Stir in the cooled shrimp mixture with the crab mixture; top with cracker crumbs and sprinkle with more Old Bay Seasoning. Bake for 30–35 minutes until the top is browned. Serves 10.

Approximate nutritional analysis per serving:
Calories 411, Protein 34 g,
Carbohydrates 19 g, Fat 22 g,
Cholesterol 185 mg, Sodium 709 mg

SPAGHETTI SQUASH

1 **spaghetti squash**
1 tbs (15 ml) **olive oil**
2 **garlic cloves, finely chopped**
fresh basil leaves, shredded
¾ cup (180 ml) **plum tomatoes,**
    cut up

Preheat oven to 375°F (190°C). Cut open squash, discard seeds, and remove the strings of squash flesh. Toss squash strings with olive oil, garlic, basil, and tomatoes. Place in shallow casserole. Bake, covered, until tender, approximately 35–40 minutes. Serves 4.

Approximate nutritional analysis per serving:
Calories 85, Protein 2 g,
Carbohydrates 12 g, Fat 4 g,
Cholesterol 0 mg, Sodium 30 mg

CORN ON THE COB

6 ears **corn**
½ cup (120 ml) **softened butter**
1 tbs (15 ml) **McCORMICK or**
    SCHILLING Season-All
    Seasoned Salt
½ tsp (3 ml) **McCORMICK or**
    SCHILLING Black Pepper

Put 6 ears corn on individual sheets of heavy-duty aluminum foil. Brush with a mixture of butter, Season-All Seasoned Salt, and black pepper. Wrap tightly. Cook on grill 20 minutes. Turn occasionally. Serves 6.

Approximate nutritional analysis per serving:
Calories 207, Protein 3 g,
Carbohydrates 17 g, Fat 16 g,
Cholesterol 41 mg, Sodium 183 mg

Opposite: Corn on the Cob

BARLEY-VEGETABLE PILAF

2 tbs (30 ml) margarine
1 medium onion, diced
4 oz (120 g) mushrooms, sliced
1 cup (240 ml) reduced-sodium
    chicken or beef broth
½ cup (120 ml) pearl barley
1 tsp (5 ml) TABASCO Pepper
    Sauce
1 medium red bell pepper, diced
1 medium zucchini, sliced

In a 10-inch skillet over medium heat, melt marargine; cook onion and mushrooms 5 minutes, stirring occasionally. Add broth, barley, and Tabasco Pepper Sauce. Over high heat, bring to boil. Reduce to low; cover and simmer 20 minutes.

Add red pepper and zucchini; cover and simmer 15–20 minutes longer or until barley is tender, stirring occasionally. Serve mixture hot or cold. Serves 4.

Approximate nutritional analysis per serving:
Calories 174, Protein 5 g,
Carbohydrates 26 g, Fat 6 g,
Cholesterol 0 mg, Sodium 96 mg

SOUTHERN RICE 'N' BLACK-EYED PEAS

1 cup (240 ml) sliced
    CALIFORNIA Ripe Olives
1 - 16 oz can (480 g) black-eyed
    peas, drained
1 cup (240 ml) seeded and diced
    tomato
3 cups (720 ml) cooked white rice
½ tsp (3 ml) garlic salt
2 tbs (30 ml) olive oil
½ cup (120 ml) minced onion
¼ cup (60 ml) minced green bell
    pepper
1 tsp (5 ml) minced garlic
1 seeded and minced jalapeño
    pepper
½ cup (120 ml) thinly sliced
    scallion greens

Combine first 5 ingredients in large bowl. Heat olive oil in small pan. Add next 4 ingredients to hot oil. Sauté 5 minutes. Add to rice mixture. Stir well. Transfer to shallow casserole dish sprayed with nonstick spray. Sprinkle scallion greens on top. Cover. Bake in preheated 350°F (180°C) oven until heated through, about 25–30 minutes. Serves 6.

Approximate nutritional analysis per serving:
Calories 275, Protein 9 g,
Carbohydrates 47 g, Fat 6 g,
Cholesterol 0 mg, Sodium 179 mg

TARTAR SAUCE

1–1¼ cups (240–295 ml)
    mayonnaise
2½ tbs (38 ml) finely chopped
    sweet pickle
1 tbs (15 ml) snipped fresh
    parsley
1½ tbs (25 ml) chopped onion
    or 1 tsp (5 ml) minced onion
1 tsp (5 ml) prepared mustard

In medium bowl, stir together all ingredients until well combined. Cover and chill if not using immediately. Yields 1½ cups.

Approximate nutritional analysis per serving:
Calories 170, Protein 2 g,
Carbohydrates 2 g, Fat 17 g,
Cholesterol 147 mg, Sodium 88 mg

Courtesy of the American Egg Board.

Opposite: Barley-Vegetable Pilaf

CRANBERRY SAUCE

1 cup (240 ml) water
1 cup (240 ml) DOMINO Sugar
3 cups (720 ml) fresh or frozen cranberries

Combine water and sugar in a saucepan, stir to dissolve sugar. Bring to a boil, add cranberries and cook until skins pop, about 8–10 minutes. Remove from heat. Cool completely at room temperature. Serve warm or chilled. Yields 2½ cups.

Approximate nutritional analysis per serving:
Calories 91, Protein < 1 g,
Carbohydrates 24 g, Fat < 1 g,
Cholesterol 0 mg, Sodium < 1 mg

Cranberry Sauce

CARROT CAKE

2 cups (480 ml) flour
2 tsp (10 ml) baking powder
1½ tsp (8 ml) ARM & HAMMER
    Baking Soda
½ tsp (3 ml) cinnamon
2 cups (480 ml) sugar
1 cup (240 ml) oil
1 cup (240 ml) egg substitute
    or **4 eggs**
2 cups (480 ml) grated carrots
½ cup (120 ml) chopped nuts
1 - 3½ oz can (105 g) coconut
1 - 8 oz can (240 g) crushed
    pineapple, drained

Preheat oven to 350°F (180°C). Grease and flour a 10-inch tube pan.

Sift dry ingredients together in a large bowl. Add oil and egg substitute and mix well. Add carrots, nuts, coconut, and pineapple and blend well. Pour into pan. Bake for 1 hour. Frost with canned cream cheese frosting, if desired.
Serves 16.

Approximate nutritional analysis per serving:
Calories 388, Protein 5 g,
Carbohydrates 57 g, Fat 13 g,
Cholesterol 8 mg, Sodium 560 mg

Carrot Cake

COUNTRY APPLE DESSERT

BASE:
1 pkg. yellow cake mix
⅓ cup (80 ml) margarine or
    butter, softened
1 egg
1 - 21 oz can (630 g) apple fruit
    pie filling

TOPPING:
½ cup (120 ml) firmly packed
    DOMINO Brown Sugar
½ cup (120 ml) chopped walnuts
½ tsp (3 ml) cinnamon
1 cup (240 ml) dairy sour cream
1 egg
1 tsp (5 ml) vanilla

Heat oven to 350°F (180°C). In large bowl, combine cake mix, margarine, and egg at low speed until crumbly. Press in ungreased 13x9-inch pan; spread with apple pie filling.

Topping: Combine brown sugar, walnuts, and cinnamon; sprinkle over apple filling. In small bowl, blend sour cream, egg, and vanilla; spoon evenly over sugar mixture. Bake for 40–50 minutes or until topping is golden brown. Serve warm or cool. Serves 12.

Approximate nutritional analysis per serving:
Calories 400, Protein 4 g,
Carbohydrates 58 g, Fat 18 g,
Cholesterol 45 mg, Sodium 380 mg

APPLE UPSIDE-DOWN CAKE

2 tbs (30 ml) butter or margarine
½ cup (120 ml) IMPERIAL Brown
    Sugar
½ cup (120 ml) chopped pecans
3 medium cooking apples, pared,
    sliced
2 tbs (30 ml) lemon juice
½ cup (120 ml) butter or
    margarine
⅔ cup (160 ml) IMPERIAL Brown
    Sugar
⅓ cup (80 ml) IMPERIAL
    Granulated Sugar
1 egg
½ tsp (3 ml) vanilla
2 cups (480 ml) all-purpose flour
½ tsp (3 ml) baking soda
1 tsp (5 ml) baking powder
½ tsp (3 ml) cinnamon
½ tsp (3 ml) salt
¼ tsp (1 ml) nutmeg
½ cup (120 ml) buttermilk
whipped cream

In 9x9-inch pan, melt 2 tbs butter; spread ½ cup Imperial Brown Sugar in bottom of pan. Sprinkle with pecans; arrange apple slices on top; cover with lemon juice and set aside. Cream ½ cup butter and remaining sugars until fluffy and light. Beat in egg and vanilla thoroughly. Combine remaining dry ingredients; add alternately with buttermilk. Spread batter over apple slices in pan. Bake in preheated oven at 375°F (190°C) for 45 minutes or until done. Place on cooling rack 10 minutes, then turn upside down on plate. Serve warm. Cut into squares and top with whipped cream. Serves 9.

Approximate nutritional analysis per serving
w/o whipped cream: Calories 423,
Protein 5 g, Carbohydrates 63 g, Fat 18 g,
Cholesterol 59 mg, Sodium 357 mg